You and Me

I Have Feelings

Angela Leeper

Heinemann Library
Chicago, Illinois

Customer Service 888-454-2279
Visit our website at www.heinemannlibrary.com

Designed by Mike Hogg (Maverick)
Printed and bound in China by South China Printing Company Limited
Photo research by Janet Lankford Moran

09 08 07 06 05
10 9 8 7 6 5 4 3 2 1

Library of Congress Cataloging-in-Publication Data
Leeper, Angela.
  I Have Feelings / Angela Leeper.
      p. cm. – (You and me)
Includes index

ISBN 1-4034-6076-0 (HB), 1-4034-6084-1(Pbk)

1. Emotions--Juvenile literature. 2. 2.Emotions. I. Title. II.Series.

BF561.L45 2004

152.4'22

2004017411

Acknowledgments
The author and publisher are grateful to the following for permission to reproduce copyright material:
Cover photograph by Ross Whitaker/The Image Bank/Getty Images
p. 4 IT Stock International/Index Stock Imagery; p. 5 Ross Whitaker/The Image Bank/Getty Images; p. 6 Michelle D. Bridwell/PhotoEdit, Inc.; pp. 7, 14 Michael Newman/Photo Edit, Inc.; pp. 8, 17 Warling Studios/Heinemann Library; p. 9 China Tourism Press/The Image Bank/Getty Images; p. 10 David Young-Wolff/Stone/Getty Images; pp. 11, 16 Janet Moran/Heinemann Library; pp. 12, 13 David Young-Wolff/Photo Edit, Inc.; p. 15 Amy Etra/Photo Edit, Inc.; p. 18 Roy Morsch/Corbis; p. 19 Bill Aron/Photo Edit, Inc.; p. 20 Mary Kate Denny/Photo Edit, Inc.; p. 21 Myrleen Ferguson Cate/Photo Edit, Inc.; pp. 22, 23 Jose Luis Pelaez, Inc./Corbis; back cover Warling Studios/Heinemann Library

Every effort has been made to contact copyright holders of any material reproduced in this book.
Any omissions will be rectified in subsequent printings if notice is given to the publisher.

Many thanks to the teachers, library media specialists, reading instructors, and educational consultants who have helped develop the Read and Learn brand.

Contents

Do You Have Feelings?

Do you sometimes feel happy?

Do you sometimes feel sad?

Those are your feelings.

Every day we have feelings.

Who Has Feelings?

Your friends have feelings.

Your parents have feelings, too.

Your classmates have feelings.

Everyone has feelings.

What Is Feeling Happy?

You may feel happy when you do well in school.

You may feel happy when you play with a friend.

You may feel happy when you celebrate a birthday.

Your family may shout, "Happy Birthday!"

What Is Feeling Sad?

You may feel sad when you cannot go outside to play.

You may feel sad when you are hurt.

You may feel sad when a friend moves away.

You may feel sad when you say, "Good-bye."

What Is Feeling Angry?

You may feel angry when you do not get what you want.

You may feel angry when you lose a game.

You may feel angry when a friend does not share with you.

You may feel angry when a friend is not honest with you.

What Is Feeling Scared?

You may feel scared when you are in the dark.

You may feel scared when you are alone.

You may feel scared in a new place.

You may feel scared on the first day of school.

How Do You Look When You Have Feelings?

When you are happy, you may smile.

When you are sad or scared, tears may roll down your face.

When you are sad, you may frown, too.

What Does It Sound Like When You Have Feelings?

When you are happy, you may laugh.

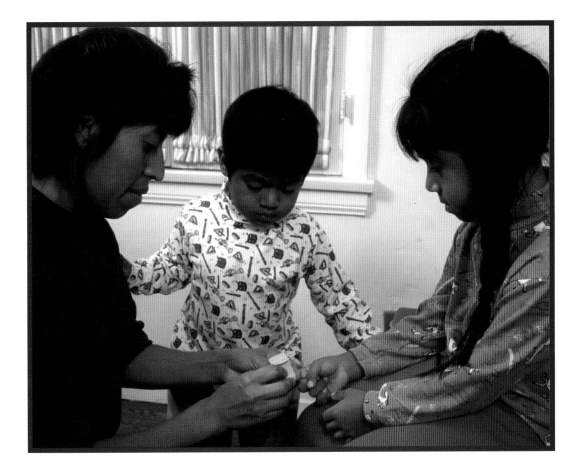

When you are sad or scared, you may cry.

Some people are quiet when they are sad.

How Do You Make Someone Feel Better?

If your friend is feeling sad, you can talk about it.

Talking about your feelings makes you feel better.

If your parents are feeling sad, you can give them a hug.

You can also tell them, "I love you."

Quiz

How does this child feel?

Answer to Quiz

This child feels happy.

Note to Parents and Teachers

Reading for information is an important part of a child's literacy development. Learning begins with a question about something. Help children think of themselves as investigators and researchers by encouraging their questions about the world around them. Each chapter in this book begins with a question. Read the question together. Look at the pictures. Talk about what you think the answer might be. Then read the text to find out if your predictions were correct. Think of other questions you could ask about the topic, and discuss where you might find the answers. Assist children in using the picture glossary and the index to practice new vocabulary and research skills.

Index